THE JIMMY WEBB
SONGBOOK

ISBN 978-1-4768-0847-5

HAL•LEONARD®
CORPORATION

7777 W. BLUEMOUND RD. P.O. BOX 13819 MILWAUKEE, WI 53213

Visit Hal Leonard Online at
www.halleonard.com

ALL I KNOW

Words and Music by
JIMMY WEBB

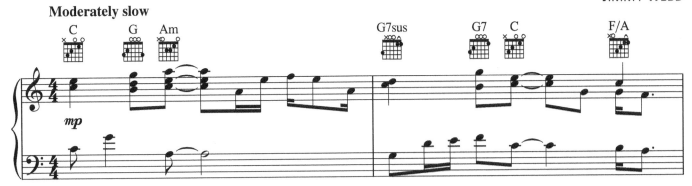

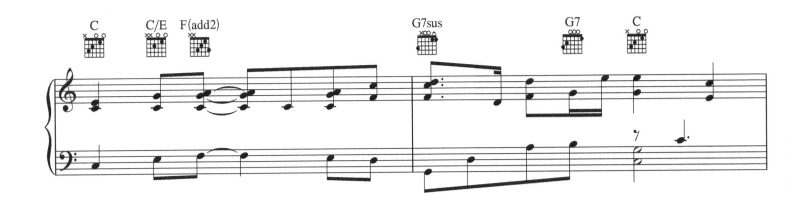

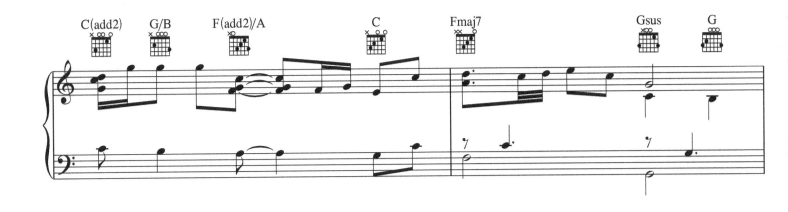

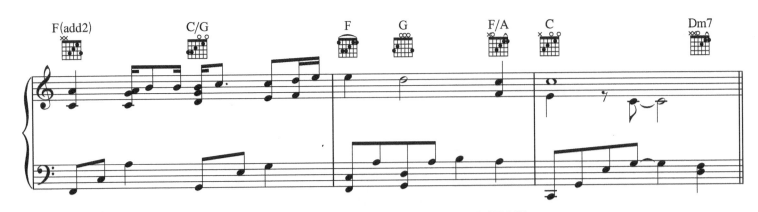

BY THE TIME I GET TO PHOENIX

Words and Music by
JIMMY WEBB

DIDN'T WE

Words and Music by
JIMMY WEBB

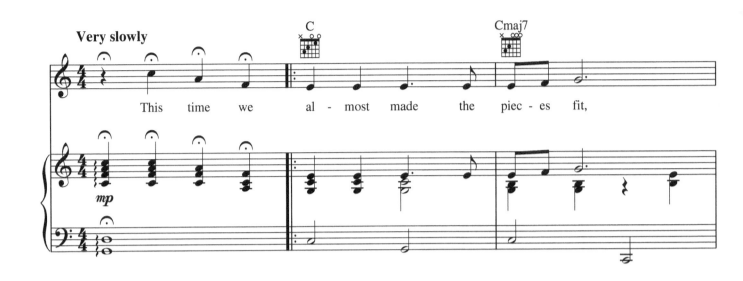

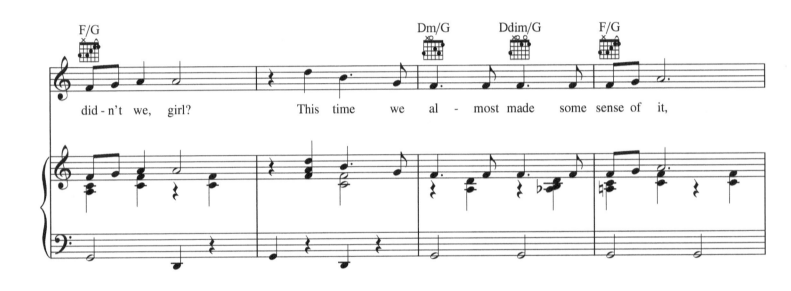

THE HIGHWAYMAN

Words and Music by
JIMMY WEBB

Additional Lyrics

2. I was a sailor,
   And I was born upon the tide,
   And with the sea I did abide.
   I sailed a schooner 'round the Horn to Mexico;
   I went aloft to furl the mainsail in a blow.
   And when the yards broke off, they say that I got killed.
   But I am living still.

3. I was a dam builder
   Across the river deep and wide,
   Where steel and water did collide.
   A place called Boulder on the wild Colorado,
   I slipped and fell into the wet concrete below.
   They buried me in that great tomb that knows no sound,
   But I am still around;
   I'll always be around, and around, and around,
   And around, and around, and around, and around.

4. I'll fly a starship
   Across the universe divide.
   And when I reach the other side,
   I'll find a place to rest my spirit if I can.
   Perhaps I may become a highwayman again,
   Or I may simply be a single drop of rain.
   But I remain.
   And I'll be back again, and again, and again,
   And again, and again, and again, and again.

GALVESTON

Words and Music by
JIMMY WEBB

MacARTHUR PARK

Words and Music by
JIMMY WEBB

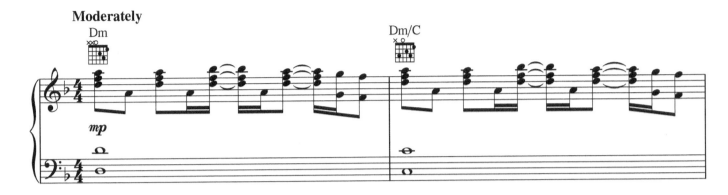

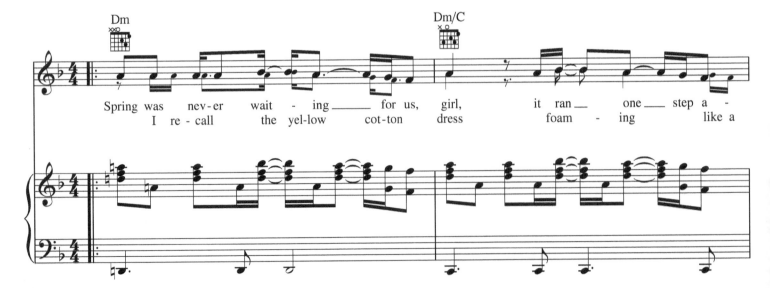

Spring was nev-er wait-ing ___ for us, girl, it ran ___ one ___ step a -
I re-call the yel-low cot-ton dress foam - ing like a

32

THE MOON IS A HARSH MISTRESS

Words and Music by
JIMMY WEBB

See her how she
flies,
shine;
gold - en sails a - cross the
good Lord, it felt so
sky.
fine,
Come e - nough to
the moon a phan - tom

UP, UP AND AWAY

Words and Music by
JIMMY WEBB

THE WORST THAT COULD HAPPEN

Words and Music by
JIM WEBB

WICHITA LINEMAN

Words and Music by
JIMMY WEBB

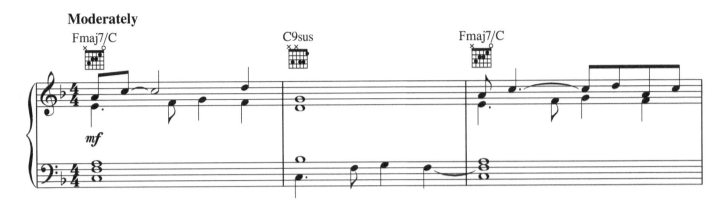

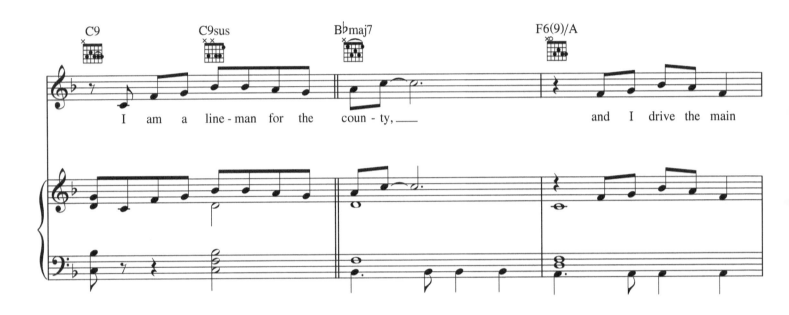

I am a line-man for the coun-ty, ___ and I drive the main

road search-in' in the sun for an-oth-er o-ver-load. ___
nev-er be ___ the same. ___